Psychic Development with Coloring Meditations

volume 1

jami gibson

BINDING LIGHT

Valencia, CA

Published by Binding Light Publications in 2015
First edition; First printing

Design and writing © 2015 Jami Gibson

JamiGibson.com

Cover Designed by Jeff Dannels
Cover frog image from Pixabay.com – user - 1293182

ISBN 978-0-9968242-0-0

dedication

This journal is dedicated to all those on their
path to enlightenment.

Pay attention to the lessons in front of you,
and most of all have fun along the way.

Introduction

The purpose of this journal is to keep all your various psychic readings organized in one place. You can have a journal for each reader you use, or a journal for a specific topic – such as one for love, another for money, another for spiritual growth, etc. The options are endless!

As someone who not only does psychic readings, but has had my fair share of them in the past, I have always taken notes and journal about the readings I received. Many times I found myself doodling while waiting for my reading or during my reading. Keeping that creative part of our brain engaged allows us to get out of our own way in the reading so we can receive a more pure and high vibration experience with our guides.

Here a couple tips for an optimal reading experience:

- ✧ Review any notes you have taken from a previous reading on your topic and reflect on what has taken place since then.
- ✧ Meditate for 5-10 minutes and focus on what you want to learn from this current reading.
- ✧ Open your journal and write your questions in the spaces provided.
- ✧ Take a deep breath and relax.

In order to help you attain and stay in that higher vibration, I have included the following for you with each reading:

- ✧ An inspirational quote.
- ✧ A couple of areas for doodling to allow you to stay in an open frame of mind.
- ✧ A mandala I have designed for a coloring meditation along with an affirmation to reflect on while you color.

Now relax and remember, if you hear something in your reading you do not like, you do have the ability to take action steps to shift things for you. You are the designer of your own experience!

(There are blank pages between reading sessions so that while you are coloring your mandalas you will not experience bleed though onto the next page.)

How to use this journal

Here are some simple guidelines to follow as you use your psychic readings journal so you can make the most out of it.

1. A Table of Contents page to keep track of your readings. You can make a note on the line of the date of the reading, who did the reading, what the purpose of the reading was, anything. This will help you to quickly find your notes at anytime.

2. The first page of each section has prompts to allow you to identify the date you had the reading done as well as who did your reading.

3. Think about what you want to focus on in your reading. What is your intention?

4. Sometimes opening up to your creative side and doodling how you are feeling allows your vibration to open up more which then makes the connection with your reader even stronger.

5. Make a note of how you are feeling before your reading. Then later come back and reflect on the information presented and how you feel about it.

6. Make a list of the questions you want to ask in your reading. There is plenty of room to make notes about the information you receive during your reading.

7. There is a section for "Action Steps" that may have been suggested to you during your reading, or an action that has intuitively come to you. Make notes of what you can do to make the most of the information from your reading.

8. An "Outcome/Follow-Up" section is included for you to come back to later to note the progress or results from your reading.

9. At the end of each section is a unique mandala designed for your reading. Use your creative side to make it unique to you. Remember, the more you stay in the high vibration of creativity, the more you stay out of your own way so the guides can assist you in your desired manifestations!

Table of contents

Fill in the blanks with your readings for later quick reference!

Cultivate the habit of being grateful for every good thing that comes to you and to give thanks continuously. And because all things have contributed to your advancement, you should include all things in your gratitude.

- Ralph Waldo Emerson (1803-1882)

My Reading

Name of Reader:_____

Phone Number & Ext.:_____

Store/Co. Name:_____

Website:_____

Date:_____

☐ In person

☐ Online

☐ Phone/Skype

My intention for this reading is...

_____

_____

_____

_____

Doodle your feelings......

How do I feel prior to this reading?

_____

_____

_____

How do I feel after this reading?

_____

_____

_____

Questions Asked & Responses

1) _____

_____

_____

_____

_____

_____

2) _____

_____

_____

_____

_____

_____

3) _____

_____

_____

_____

_____

_____

4) _____

_____

_____

_____

_____

_____

Additional Notes/Summary

_____

_____

_____

_____

_____

_____

_____

_____

_____

_____

_____

_____

_____

_____

_____

_____

_____

_____

_____

_____

Keep doodling!!

Action Steps

- [ ] Ask & let it go
- [ ] Get outside, hug a tree
- [ ] Have fun! *(dance, play, etc.)*
- [ ] Journal
- [ ] Meditate

- [ ] Release anxiety & worry
- [ ] Visualize
- [ ] _____
- [ ] _____
- [ ] _____

More specific action steps...

_____

_____

_____

_____

_____

_____

_____

_____

Outcome/Follow-Up

_____

_____

_____

_____

_____

_____

_____

_____

_____

 I am learning to stay in the present moment and appreciating that which is all around me.

14

All that we are is a result of what we have thought.

The mind is everything.

What we think we become.

- Buddha (624BC - 543BC)

My Reading

Name of Reader:_____

Phone Number & Ext.:_____

Store/Co. Name:_____

Website:_____

Date:_____

☐   In person

☐   Online

☐   Phone/Skype

My intention for this reading is...

_____

_____

_____

_____

Doodle your feelings......

How do I feel prior to this reading?

_____

_____

_____

How do I feel after this reading?

_____

_____

_____

Questions Asked & Responses

1)_____
_____
_____
_____
_____
_____

2)_____
_____
_____
_____
_____
_____

3)_____
_____
_____
_____
_____

4)_____
_____
_____
_____
_____

Additional Notes/Summary

_____
_____
_____
_____
_____
_____
_____
_____
_____
_____
_____
_____
_____
_____
_____
_____
_____
_____
_____
_____

Keep doodling!!

Action Steps

☐ Ask & let it go

☐ Get outside, hug a tree

☐ Have fun! *(dance, play, etc.)*

☐ Journal

☐ Meditate

☐ Release anxiety & worry

☐ Visualize

☐ _____

☐ _____

☐ _____

More specific action steps...

_____

_____

_____

_____

_____

_____

_____

Outcome/Follow-Up

_____

_____

_____

_____

_____

_____

_____

_____

 I am deeply grateful for the beauty and wisdom of all those around me.

When you arise in the morning,
think of what a precious privilege it is to be alive...
To breathe... To think... To Enjoy... To Love.

- Marcus Aurelius (121-180)

My Reading

Name of Reader:_____

Phone Number & Ext.:_____

Store/Co. Name:_____

Website:_____

Date:_____

☐   In person

☐   Online

☐   Phone/Skype

My intention for this reading is...

_____

_____

_____

_____

Doodle your feelings......

How do I feel prior to this reading?

_____

_____

_____

How do I feel after this reading?

_____

_____

_____

Questions Asked & Responses

1)_____

_____

_____

_____

_____

_____

2)_____

_____

_____

_____

_____

_____

3)_____

_____

_____

_____

_____

_____

4)_____

_____

_____

_____

_____

_____

Additional Notes/Summary

_____
_____
_____
_____
_____
_____
_____
_____
_____
_____
_____
_____
_____
_____
_____
_____
_____

Keep doodling!!

Action Steps

- [ ] Ask & let it go
- [ ] Get outside, hug a tree
- [ ] Have fun! (dance, play, etc.)
- [ ] Journal
- [ ] Meditate

- [ ] Release anxiety & worry
- [ ] Visualize
- [ ] _____
- [ ] _____
- [ ] _____

More specific action steps...

_____

_____

_____

_____

_____

_____

_____

Outcome/Follow-Up

_____

_____

_____

_____

_____

_____

_____

_____

 I know everyday my choices are taking me to the place where I need to be.

It's impossible," said Pride.

"It's risky," said Experience.

"It's pointless," said Reason.

"Give it a try," whispered the Heart.

- Unknown

My Reading

Name of Reader:_____

Phone Number & Ext.:_____

Store/Co. Name:_____

Website:_____

Date:_____

☐ In person

☐ Online

☐ Phone/Skype

My intention for this reading is...

_____

_____

_____

_____

Doodle your feelings......

How do I feel prior to this reading?

_____

_____

How do I feel after this reading?

_____

_____

_____

Questions Asked & Responses

1) _____

_____

_____

_____

_____

_____

2) _____

_____

_____

_____

_____

_____

3) _____

_____

_____

_____

_____

_____

4) _____

_____

_____

_____

_____

_____

Additional Notes/Summary

_____

_____

_____

_____

_____

_____

_____

_____

_____

_____

_____

_____

_____

_____

_____

_____

_____

_____

_____

Keep doodling!!

Action Steps

- ☐ Ask & let it go
- ☐ Get outside, hug a tree
- ☐ Have fun! (dance, play, etc.)
- ☐ Journal
- ☐ Meditate

- ☐ Release anxiety & worry
- ☐ Visualize
- ☐ _____
- ☐ _____
- ☐ _____

More specific action steps...

_____
_____
_____
_____
_____
_____
_____

Outcome/Follow-Up

_____
_____
_____
_____
_____
_____
_____
_____

 I am releasing old habits of thoughts and embracing new opportunities.

We are disturbed, not by what happens to us,
but by our thoughts about what happens.

- Epictetus (55-135)

My Reading

Name of Reader:_____

Phone Number & Ext.:_____

Store/Co. Name:_____

Website:_____

Date:_____

☐ In person

☐ Online

☐ Phone/Skype

My intention for this reading is...

_____

_____

_____

_____

Doodle your feelings......

How do I feel prior to this reading?

_____

_____

_____

How do I feel after this reading?

_____

_____

_____

Questions Asked & Responses

1)_____

_____

_____

_____

_____

_____

2)_____

_____

_____

_____

_____

_____

3)_____

_____

_____

_____

_____

_____

4)_____

_____

_____

_____

_____

_____

Additional Notes/Summary

_____

_____

_____

_____

_____

_____

_____

_____

_____

_____

_____

_____

_____

_____

_____

_____

_____

_____

Keep doodling!!

Action Steps

- [ ] Ask & let it go
- [ ] Get outside, hug a tree
- [ ] Have fun! *(dance, play, etc.)*
- [ ] Journal
- [ ] Meditate
- [ ] Release anxiety & worry
- [ ] Visualize
- [ ] _____
- [ ] _____
- [ ] _____

More specific action steps...

_____
_____
_____
_____
_____
_____
_____

Outcome/Follow-Up

_____
_____
_____
_____
_____
_____
_____
_____
_____

 I am tickled everyday by things around me.

Painful as it may be, a significant emotional event can be the catalyst for choosing a direction that serves us more effectively. Look for the learning.

- Louise May Alcott (1832 - 1888)

My Reading

Name of Reader:_____

Phone Number & Ext.:_____

Store/Co. Name:_____

Website:_____

Date:_____

☐ In person

☐ Online

☐ Phone/Skype

My intention for this reading is...

_____

_____

_____

_____

Doodle your feelings......

How do I feel prior to this reading?

_____

_____

_____

How do I feel after this reading?

_____

_____

_____

Questions Asked & Responses

1) _____

_____

_____

_____

_____

_____

2) _____

_____

_____

_____

_____

_____

3) _____

_____

_____

_____

_____

_____

4) _____

_____

_____

_____

_____

_____

Additional Notes/Summary

_____

_____

_____

_____

_____

_____

_____

_____

_____

_____

_____

_____

_____

_____

_____

_____

_____

_____

Keep doodling!!

Action Steps

- [ ] Ask & let it go
- [ ] Get outside, hug a tree
- [ ] Have fun! (dance, play, etc.)
- [ ] Journal
- [ ] Meditate

- [ ] Release anxiety & worry
- [ ] Visualize
- [ ] _____
- [ ] _____
- [ ] _____

More specific action steps...

_____

_____

_____

_____

_____

_____

_____

Outcome/Follow-Up

_____

_____

_____

_____

_____

_____

_____

_____

 I am creating an amazing life for myself.

Whether the events in our life are good or bad,
greatly depends on the way we perceive them.

- Michel de Montaigne (1533-1592)

My Reading

Name of Reader:_____

Phone Number & Ext.:_____

Store/Co. Name:_____

Website:_____

Date:_____

☐ In person

☐ Online

☐ Phone/Skype

My intention for this reading is...

_____

_____

_____

_____

Doodle your feelings......

How do I feel prior to this reading?

_____

_____

How do I feel after this reading?

_____

_____

_____

Questions Asked & Responses

1)_____

_____

_____

_____

_____

2)_____

_____

_____

_____

_____

3)_____

_____

_____

_____

_____

4)_____

_____

_____

_____

_____

Additional Notes/Summary

_____

_____

_____

_____

_____

_____

_____

_____

_____

_____

_____

_____

_____

_____

_____

_____

_____

_____

_____

_____

Keep doodling!!

Action Steps

- [ ] Ask & let it go
- [ ] Get outside, hug a tree
- [ ] Have fun! (dance, play, etc.)
- [ ] Journal
- [ ] Meditate

- [ ] Release anxiety & worry
- [ ] Visualize
- [ ] _____
- [ ] _____
- [ ] _____

More specific action steps...

_____
_____
_____
_____
_____
_____
_____

Outcome/Follow-Up

_____
_____
_____
_____
_____
_____
_____
_____

 I am open to happiness in all ways
that it is available.

A problem is a problem only when you think it is a problem.

In the perspective of your soul...

Every problem is an opportunity to achieve a higher consciousness.

                                               - Unknown

My Reading

Name of Reader:_____

Phone Number & Ext.:_____

Store/Co. Name:_____

Website:_____

Date:_____

☐ In person

☐ Online

☐ Phone/Skype

My intention for this reading is...

_____

_____

_____

_____

Doodle your feelings......

How do I feel prior to this reading?

_____

_____

How do I feel after this reading?

_____

_____

_____

Questions Asked & Responses

1) _____

_____

_____

_____

_____

_____

2) _____

_____

_____

_____

_____

_____

3) _____

_____

_____

_____

_____

4) _____

_____

_____

_____

_____

_____

Additional Notes/Summary

_____
_____
_____
_____
_____
_____
_____
_____
_____
_____
_____
_____
_____
_____
_____
_____
_____
_____
_____
_____
_____

Keep doodling!!

Action Steps

- [ ] Ask & let it go
- [ ] Get outside, hug a tree
- [ ] Have fun! (dance, play, etc.)
- [ ] Journal
- [ ] Meditate
- [ ] Release anxiety & worry
- [ ] Visualize
- [ ] _____
- [ ] _____
- [ ] _____

More specific action steps...

_____

_____

_____

_____

_____

_____

_____

Outcome/Follow-Up

_____

_____

_____

_____

_____

_____

_____

_____

 I am trusting in the universe that all is well.

70

You wander from room to room hunting for the diamond necklace that is already around your neck.

-Jalal uddin Rumi (1207-1273)

My Reading

Name of Reader:_____

Phone Number & Ext.:_____

Store/Co. Name:_____

Website:_____

Date:_____

☐ In person

☐ Online

☐ Phone/Skype

My intention for this reading is...

_____

_____

_____

_____

Doodle your feelings......

How do I feel prior to this reading?

_____

_____

_____

How do I feel after this reading?

_____

_____

_____

Questions Asked & Responses

1)_____

_____

_____

_____

_____

_____

2)_____

_____

_____

_____

_____

_____

3)_____

_____

_____

_____

_____

_____

4)_____

_____

_____

_____

_____

_____

Additional Notes/Summary

_____

_____

_____

_____

_____

_____

_____

_____

_____

_____

_____

_____

_____

_____

_____

_____

_____

_____

_____

_____

Keep doodling!!

Action Steps

- [ ] Ask & let it go
- [ ] Get outside, hug a tree
- [ ] Have fun! *(dance, play, etc.)*
- [ ] Journal
- [ ] Meditate

- [ ] Release anxiety & worry
- [ ] Visualize
- [ ] _____
- [ ] _____
- [ ] _____

More specific action steps...

_____
_____
_____
_____
_____
_____
_____
_____

Outcome/Follow-Up

_____
_____
_____
_____
_____
_____
_____
_____
_____

 I have the ability to take any path I desire.

He that is discontented in one place
will seldom be happy in another.

- Aesop (620BC – 564BC)

My Reading

Name of Reader:_____

Phone Number & Ext.:_____

Store/Co. Name:_____

Website:_____

Date:_____

☐ In person

☐ Online

☐ Phone/Skype

My intention for this reading is...

_____

_____

_____

_____

Doodle your feelings......

How do I feel prior to this reading?

_____

_____

_____

How do I feel after this reading?

_____

_____

_____

Questions Asked & Responses

1)_____

_____

_____

_____

_____

_____

2)_____

_____

_____

_____

_____

_____

3)_____

_____

_____

_____

_____

_____

4)_____

_____

_____

_____

_____

_____

Additional Notes/Summary

_____

_____

_____

_____

_____

_____

_____

_____

_____

_____

_____

_____

_____

_____

_____

_____

_____

_____

_____

Keep doodling!!

Action Steps

- [ ] Ask & let it go
- [ ] Get outside, hug a tree
- [ ] Have fun! (dance, play, etc.)
- [ ] Journal
- [ ] Meditate
- [ ] Release anxiety & worry
- [ ] Visualize
- [ ] _____
- [ ] _____
- [ ] _____

More specific action steps...

_____
_____
_____
_____
_____
_____
_____
_____

Outcome/Follow-Up

_____
_____
_____
_____
_____
_____
_____
_____

 I am appreciating the opportunities in every situation.

The secret of change is to focus all of your energy, not on fighting the old, but on building the new.

- Socrates (470BC – 399BC)

My Reading

Name of Reader:_____

Phone Number & Ext.:_____

Store/Co. Name:_____

Website:_____

Date:_____

☐   In person

☐   Online

☐   Phone/Skype

My intention for this reading is...

_____

_____

_____

_____

Doodle your feelings......

How do I feel prior to this reading?

_____

_____

_____

How do I feel after this reading?

_____

_____

_____

Questions Asked & Responses

1)_____

_____

_____

_____

_____

_____

2)_____

_____

_____

_____

_____

_____

3)_____

_____

_____

_____

_____

_____

4)_____

_____

_____

_____

_____

_____

Additional Notes/Summary

_____
_____
_____
_____
_____
_____
_____
_____
_____
_____
_____
_____
_____
_____
_____
_____
_____
_____
_____

Keep doodling!!

Action Steps

- [ ] Ask & let it go
- [ ] Get outside, hug a tree
- [ ] Have fun! *(dance, play, etc.)*
- [ ] Journal
- [ ] Meditate

- [ ] Release anxiety & worry
- [ ] Visualize
- [ ] _____
- [ ] _____
- [ ] _____

More specific action steps...

_____

_____

_____

_____

_____

_____

_____

_____

Outcome/Follow-Up

_____

_____

_____

_____

_____

_____

_____

_____

 I have great knowledge.

Your task is not to seek for love, but merely to seek and find all the barriers within yourself that you have built against it.

- Jalal Uddin Rumi (1207-1273)

My Reading

Name of Reader:_____

Phone Number & Ext.:_____

Store/Co. Name:_____

Website:_____

Date:_____

☐ In person

☐ Online

☐ Phone/Skype

My intention for this reading is...

_____

_____

_____

_____

Doodle your feelings......

How do I feel prior to this reading?

_____

_____

How do I feel after this reading?

_____

_____

_____

Questions Asked & Responses

1)_____

_____

_____

_____

_____

2)_____

_____

_____

_____

_____

3)_____

_____

_____

_____

_____

4)_____

_____

_____

_____

_____

Additional Notes/Summary

_____

_____

_____

_____

_____

_____

_____

_____

_____

_____

_____

_____

_____

_____

_____

_____

_____

_____

Keep doodling!!

Action Steps

- [ ] Ask & let it go
- [ ] Get outside, hug a tree
- [ ] Have fun! *(dance, play, etc.)*
- [ ] Journal
- [ ] Meditate
- [ ] Release anxiety & worry
- [ ] Visualize
- [ ] _____
- [ ] _____
- [ ] _____

More specific action steps...

_____
_____
_____
_____
_____
_____
_____
_____

Outcome/Follow-Up

_____
_____
_____
_____
_____
_____
_____
_____

 I know that I hold all the answers I need about my own well being.

People are just as happy as
they make up their minds to be.

- Abraham Lincoln (1809-1865)

My Reading

Name of Reader:_____

Phone Number & Ext.:_____

Store/Co. Name:_____

Website:_____

Date:_____

☐ In person

☐ Online

☐ Phone/Skype

My intention for this reading is...

_____

_____

_____

_____

Doodle your feelings......

How do I feel prior to this reading?

_____

_____

_____

How do I feel after this reading?

_____

_____

_____

Questions Asked & Responses

1)_____

_____

_____

_____

_____

_____

2)_____

_____

_____

_____

_____

_____

3)_____

_____

_____

_____

_____

_____

4)_____

_____

_____

_____

_____

_____

Additional Notes/Summary

_____

_____

_____

_____

_____

_____

_____

_____

_____

_____

_____

_____

_____

_____

_____

_____

_____

_____

_____

_____

Keep doodling!!

Action Steps

- [ ] Ask & let it go
- [ ] Get outside, hug a tree
- [ ] Have fun! (dance, play, etc.)
- [ ] Journal
- [ ] Meditate

- [ ] Release anxiety & worry
- [ ] Visualize
- [ ] _____
- [ ] _____
- [ ] _____

More specific action steps...

_____
_____
_____
_____
_____
_____
_____

Outcome/Follow-Up

_____
_____
_____
_____
_____
_____
_____
_____

 I am practicing patience and acceptance.

Holding on to anger is like grasping a hot coal with the intent of throwing it at someone else...YOU are the one who gets burned.

- Buddha (624BC - 543BC)

My Reading

Name of Reader:_____

Phone Number & Ext.:_____

Store/Co. Name:_____

Website:_____

Date:_____

☐　In person

☐　Online

☐　Phone/Skype

My intention for this reading is...

_____

_____

_____

_____

Doodle your feelings......

How do I feel prior to this reading?

_____

_____

_____

How do I feel after this reading?

_____

_____

_____

Questions Asked & Responses

1) _____

_____

_____

_____

_____

_____

2) _____

_____

_____

_____

_____

_____

3) _____

_____

_____

_____

_____

4) _____

_____

_____

_____

_____

Additional Notes/Summary

_____

_____

_____

_____

_____

_____

_____

_____

_____

_____

_____

_____

_____

_____

_____

_____

_____

_____

_____

Keep doodling!!

Action Steps

- [ ] Ask & let it go
- [ ] Get outside, hug a tree
- [ ] Have fun! (dance, play, etc.)
- [ ] Journal
- [ ] Meditate

- [ ] Release anxiety & worry
- [ ] Visualize
- [ ] _____
- [ ] _____
- [ ] _____

More specific action steps...

_____

_____

_____

_____

_____

_____

_____

Outcome/Follow-Up

_____

_____

_____

_____

_____

_____

_____

 I am forever thankful for the miracles in my life.

Without winter... there can be no spring.
Without mistakes... there can be no learning.
Without doubts... there can be no faith.
Without fears... there can be no courage.
My mistakes, my fears and my doubts are my path to
Wisdom, Faith and Courage.

- Unknown

My Reading

Name of Reader:_____

Phone Number & Ext.:_____

Store/Co. Name:_____

Website:_____

Date:_____

☐ In person

☐ Online

☐ Phone/Skype

My intention for this reading is...

_____

_____

_____

_____

Doodle your feelings......

How do I feel prior to this reading?

_____

_____

_____

How do I feel after this reading?

_____

_____

_____

Questions Asked & Responses

1) _____

_____

_____

_____

_____

_____

2) _____

_____

_____

_____

_____

_____

3) _____

_____

_____

_____

_____

4) _____

_____

_____

_____

_____

Additional Notes/Summary

_____

_____

_____

_____

_____

_____

_____

_____

_____

_____

_____

_____

_____

_____

_____

_____

_____

_____

_____

Keep doodling!!

Action Steps

- ☐ Ask & let it go
- ☐ Get outside, hug a tree
- ☐ Have fun! (dance, play, etc.)
- ☐ Journal
- ☐ Meditate

- ☐ Release anxiety & worry
- ☐ Visualize
- ☐ _____
- ☐ _____
- ☐ _____

More specific action steps...

_____
_____
_____
_____
_____
_____
_____
_____

Outcome/Follow-Up

_____
_____
_____
_____
_____
_____
_____
_____
_____

 I am embracing change.

For every minute you are angry, you lose sixty seconds of happiness.

- Ralph Waldo Emerson (1803-1882)

My Reading

Name of Reader:_____

Phone Number & Ext.:_____

Store/Co. Name:_____

Website:_____

Date:_____

☐ In person

☐ Online

☐ Phone/Skype

My intention for this reading is...

_____

_____

_____

_____

Doodle your feelings......

How do I feel prior to this reading?

_____

_____

How do I feel after this reading?

_____

_____

_____

Questions Asked & Responses

1) _____

_____

_____

_____

_____

_____

2) _____

_____

_____

_____

_____

_____

3) _____

_____

_____

_____

_____

_____

4) _____

_____

_____

_____

_____

_____

Additional Notes/Summary

_____

_____

_____

_____

_____

_____

_____

_____

_____

_____

_____

_____

_____

_____

_____

_____

_____

_____

Keep doodling!!

Action Steps

- [ ] Ask & let it go
- [ ] Get outside, hug a tree
- [ ] Have fun! *(dance, play, etc.)*
- [ ] Journal
- [ ] Meditate

- [ ] Release anxiety & worry
- [ ] Visualize
- [ ] _____
- [ ] _____
- [ ] _____

More specific action steps...

_____

_____

_____

_____

_____

_____

_____

_____

Outcome/Follow-Up

_____

_____

_____

_____

_____

_____

_____

_____

_____

 I feel connected to all around me.

A little about jami gibson

Jami Gibson is an intuitive empathic, clairsentient and clairvoyant. In every day terms:

- **Empathic** she can actually FEEL what another person is experiencing.

- **Clairsentient** she receives strong sensations and impressions, both emotional and physical, from the energies and guides around her.

- **Clairvoyant** she is able to see the energies around a person which allows her to experience what that person has gone through, what feelings they commonly have, their outlook on life as well as other characteristics about them.

Jami has counseled hundreds of people from around the world with her intuitive gifts. You can read more about Jami's intuitive work at

www.ReadingsByJami.com

In addition to doing psychic readings, Jami has many journals and coloring books she has designed, which can be found on her website www.JamiGibson.com, on Amazon and other online retailers, as well in many stores.

She loves colors and coloring and has a life long obsession with Crayola Crayons (ask her kids how embarrassing that has been all their lives!)

Look for more journals on new topics and coloring books coming soon!

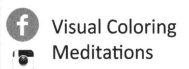

CPSIA information can be obtained
at www.ICGtesting.com
Printed in the USA
BVHW022159160623
666060BV00010B/1551